HIT SONGS FOR TWO

Arrangements by Peter Deneff

ISBN 978-1-5400-1277-7

HAL•LEONARD®

7777 W. BLUEMOUND RD. P.O. BOX 13819 MILWAUKEE, WI 53213

Visit Hal Leonard Online at
www.halleonard.com

CONTENTS

ALL ABOUT THAT BASS

CLARINETS

Words and Music by KEVIN KADISH
and MEGHAN TRAINOR

Moderately

ALL OF ME

CLARINETS

Words and Music by JOHN STEPHENS
and TOBY GAD

Moderately

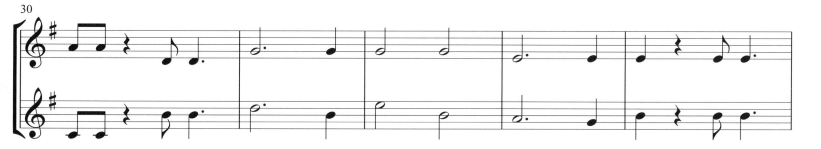

BRAVE

CLARINETS

Words and Music by SARA BAREILLES
and JACK ANTONOFF

Moderately

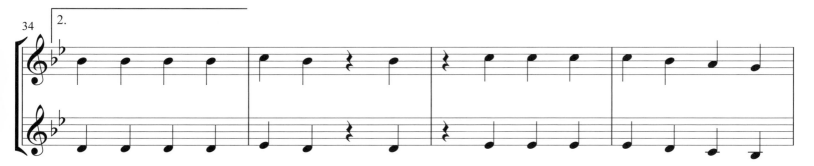

BUDAPEST

CLARINETS

Words and Music by GEORGE BARNETT
and JOEL POTT

21

25

29

33

37
D.C. al Coda

CODA

CAN'T STOP THE FEELING
from TROLLS

CLARINETS

Words and Music by JUSTIN TIMBERLAKE,
MAX MARTIN and SHELLBACK

Moderately

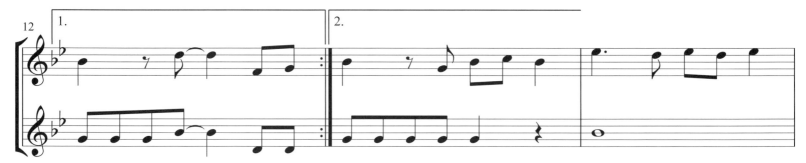

GRENADE

CLARINETS

Words and Music by BRUNO MARS,
ARI LEVINE, PHILIP LAWRENCE,
BRODY BROWN, CLAUDE KELLY
and ANDREW WYATT

HEY, SOUL SISTER

CLARINETS

Words and Music by PAT MONAHAN,
ESPEN LIND and AMUND BJORKLUND

Moderately

HOME

CLARINETS

Words and Music by GREG HOLDEN
and DREW PEARSON

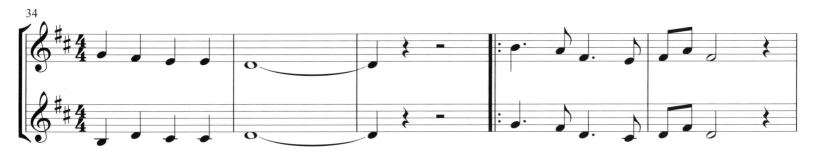

I WILL WAIT

CLARINETS

Words and Music by
MUMFORD & SONS

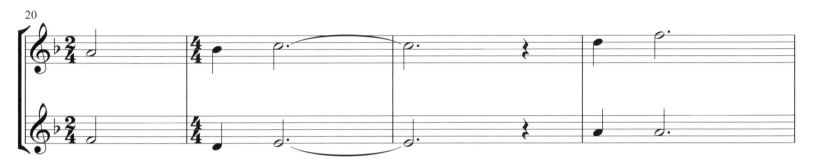

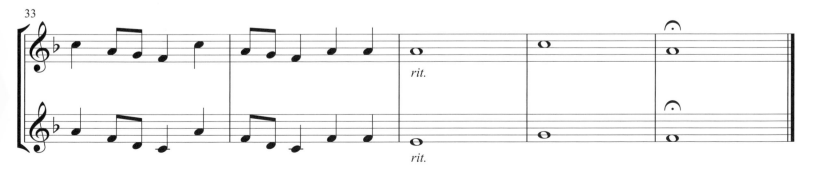

LET HER GO

CLARINETS

Words and Music by
MICHAEL DAVID ROSENBERG

Moderately

D.S. al Coda

CODA

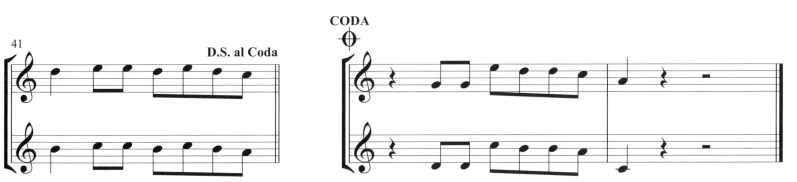

LET IT GO

CLARINETS

Words and Music by JAMES BAY
and PAUL BARRY

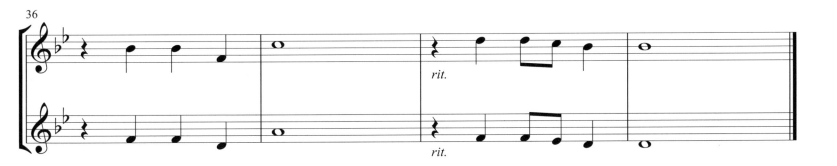

100 YEARS

CLARINETS

Words and Music by
JOHN ONDRASIK

Moderately

rit.

rit.

POKER FACE

CLARINETS

Words and Music by STEFANI GERMANOTTA
and RedOne

ROYALS

Clarinets

Words and Music by ELLA YELICH-O'CONNOR
and JOEL LITTLE

Moderately

(small note optional)

SAY SOMETHING

CLARINETS

Words and Music by IAN AXEL,
CHAD VACCARINO and MIKE CAMPBELL

Moderately slow

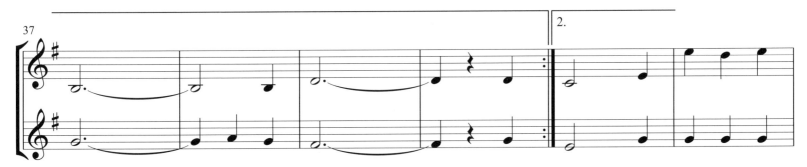

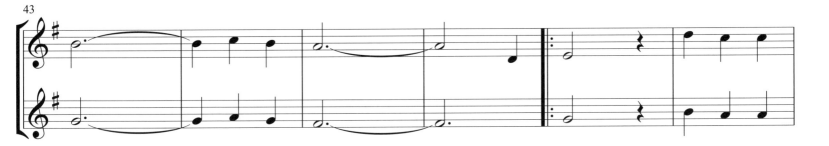

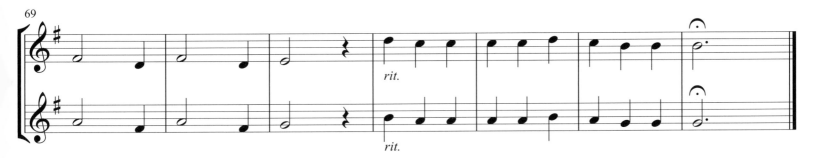

SHAKE IT OFF

CLARINETS

Words and Music by TAYLOR SWIFT,
MAX MARTIN and SHELLBACK

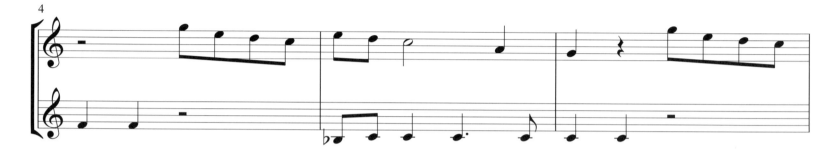

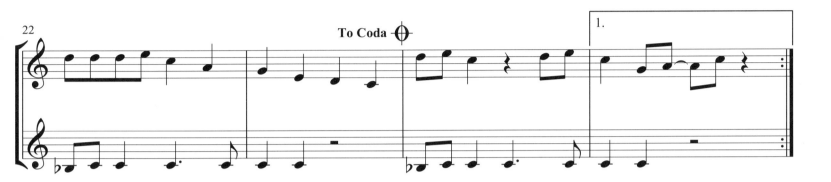

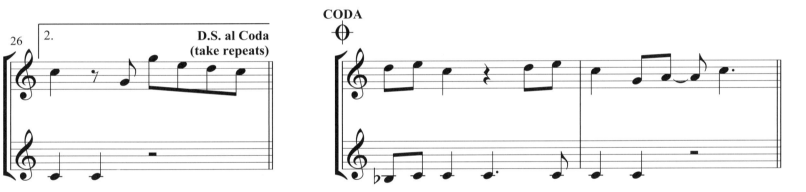

SHAPE OF YOU

CLARINETS

Words and Music by ED SHEERAN,
KEVIN BRIGGS, KANDI BURRUSS,
TAMEKA COTTLE, STEVE MAC
and JOHNNY McDAID

Moderately fast

SKYFALL

from the Motion Picture SKYFALL

CLARINETS

Words and Music by ADELE ADKINS
and PAUL EPWORTH

Moderately slow

SOME NIGHTS

CLARINETS

Words and Music by JEFF BHASKER,
ANDREW DOST, JACK ANTONOFF
and NATE RUESS

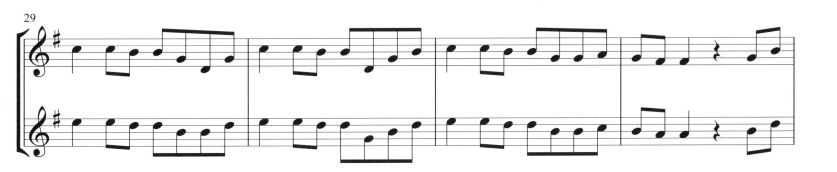

STAY WITH ME

Clarinets

Words and Music by SAM SMITH,
JAMES NAPIER, WILLIAM EDWARD PHILLIPS,
TOM PETTY and JEFF LYNNE

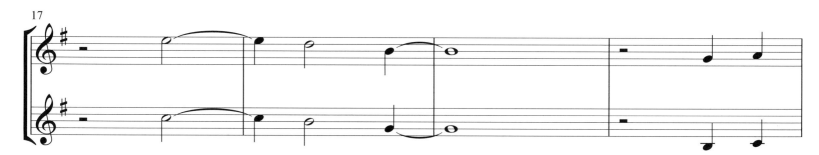

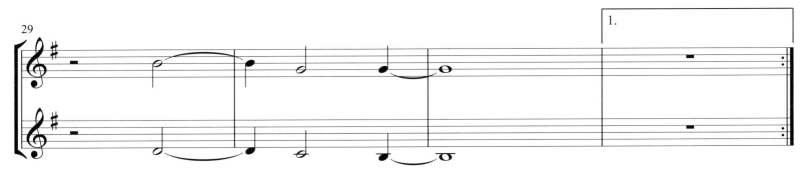

STORY OF MY LIFE

CLARINETS

Words and Music by JAMIE SCOTT,
JOHN HENRY RYAN, JULIAN BUNETTA,
HARRY STYLES, LIAM PAYNE, LOUIS TOMLINSON,
NIALL HORAN and ZAIN MALIK

VIVA LA VIDA

CLARINETS

Words and Music by GUY BERRYMAN,
JON BUCKLAND, WILL CHAMPION
and CHRIS MARTIN

Moderately

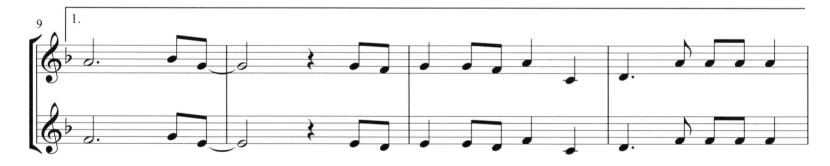

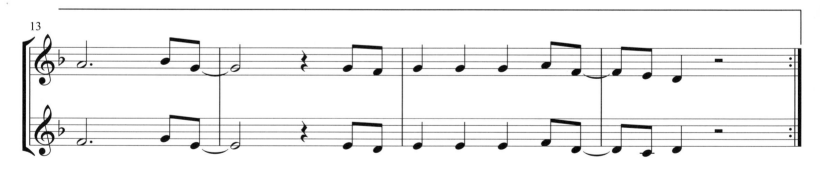

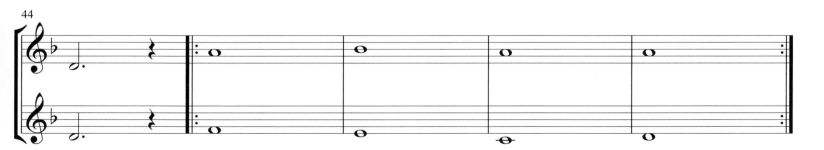

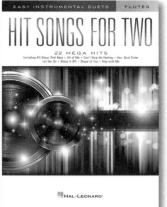